NEW AND RENEWED

Brian Lynch was born in Dublin in 1945. His first book, *Endsville* (1967), was shared with Paul Durcan, while his play, *Crooked in the Car Seat*, was nominated for a Harvey Award in the 1979 Dublin Theatre Festival. *Caught in a Free State*, a 1984 four-part RTÉ/Channel 4 series about German spies in Ireland during World War II, won a Jacobs Award and the Banff International TV Festival Award for best drama. A feature film, *Love and Rage*, was directed by Cathal Black in 1999. He compiled and edited a book about the artist Tony O'Malley, published in 1994 by the Butler Gallery, Kilkenny and the Scolar Press, London, and he has recently completed a novel, *The Winner of Sorrow*, about the poet William Cowper. He was elected to Aosdána in 1985, nominated by Michael Hartnett and Samuel Beckett.

NEW AND RENEWED
Poems 1967–2004

BRIAN LYNCH

**NEW
ISLAND**

New and Renewed
First published 2004
by New Island
2 Brookside
Dundrum Road
Dublin 14
www.newisland.ie

ISBN 1 904301 56 8

British Library Cataloguing in Publication Data. A CIP catalogue record for this book is
available from the British Library.

Typeset by New Island
Cover design by New Island
Printed in Ireland by ColourBooks

New Island received financial assistance from
The Arts Council (An Chomhairle Ealaíon), Dublin, Ireland.

10 9 8 7 6 5 4 3 2 1

For Clare

ALSO BY BRIAN LYNCH

Endsville (shared with Paul Durcan), New Writers Press,
Dublin, 1967
No Die Cast, New Writers Press, 1969
Outside The Pheasantry, Gorey Arts Press, Wexford, 1975
Perpetual Star, Raven Arts Press, Dublin, 1981
Beds Of Down, Raven Arts Press, 1983
Paul Celan: 65 Poems, Raven Arts Press, 1986, translated
from the German with Peter Jankowsky
Voices From The Nettle Way, Raven Arts Press, 1989
Easter Snow, Salmon Press and die horen, Bremen, 1993,
photographs of Clare Island by Peter Jankowsky who also
translated the poems
Playtime, RHA Gallagher Gallery and New Island Books,
Dublin, 1997, poems about paintings by Gene Lambert

CONTENTS

Acknowledgements

I wish to express my appreciation to Dermot Bolger, founder of Raven Arts Press, whose support over many years has been invaluable; to the Corporation of Yaddo, New York, where I held the Howard Moss Poetry Residency in 2003; and to Aosdána, without which this book would not exist in its present form.

FIRST POEM

I went out with nowhere to go,
Past the houses
And well past the snow.
The river in the reeds
Beneath the Tolka bridge
Slowed down and froze,
And I too waited
On silence an age.

The Wooden Church was closed
And yet its bell began to chime
The Seven Dolours of Glasnevin.
I thought of God, waylaid by time.
He could not be something, so
He must be nothing.
There was no heaven,
There was only the snow.

Beyond the city, still as death,
The sea at Ireland's Eye
Let out its breath.
A child was being born
That would not cry.
The baby crowed
And I began to shiver
Outside of the houses
Alone in the snow.

The windows glowed
As if they knew.
The sky, grown clear, allowed
The stars resume their dance

In the river,
And the moon came out too,
For the child was stubborn still
That laughed with chance
On Mobhi Hill.

I went home with nowhere to go,
Past the houses
And well, well past the snow.

SEA GHOST

The night we came back to meet
Our mother for the first time
After our father's funeral,
She was sitting in the sitting room
In an unusual chair not near the fire.

Her hair had turned white and thin,
Her features were made of cuttle-bone,
And her eyes had stayed down there.

We kissed and made our way across
The deep red patterned carpet to the fire.

Sometimes even the most hardened fisherman
Will see what's in his nets and turn aside
And say, for god's sake, throw it back again.

THE SNOW DOME

A snowstorm in a globe of glass,
A blizzard blowing through the house.
I was ill, in my parents' bed.
The coverlet was silken stuff,
Its colour, eau-de-nil, was thought.
The furniture obeyed its laws,
The Nile, the mirror, silvered off.

My father was not long since dead,
My mother an Egyptian queen.
The dome was blue. I was cold and hot.
The snowflakes, thick as little sheep,
Were falling on not from the sky.
They teemed, like me, set loose and caught.

I sank into a fevered sleep
And dreamt beneath the eiderdown
That if I didn't rise, I'd drown.

The water froze, the fever broke,
The boat came up, and then I woke.
The room was cool and green and dry.

But still a long way down I guessed
The dome is always solid glass.

MAYDAY

I climbed the wardrobe in
My parents' room and dived
Onto the silken bed,
Somersaulting as I fell
And bouncing to my feet again.
My father was still dead.
I flew around like a robin.
And then one time, my brother
Laughing in the well
The lamplight made,
My knee gave out. Our mother
Was at first annoyed,
Or as we said, vexed:
What's going on up there,
She cried from far downstairs.
As pain does not, I didn't care.
I didn't cry for her.
The cartilage had looped itself
Around the bone and locked.
I clutched it in, to fix it,
The pain grew worse.
How long until I knew
I had to straighten it,
To hurt myself the most,
To make it stop?
It seemed as long as life.
And so I crept into their bed,
Half a ghost, half an orphan with,
For wing, a buckling knee,
Knowing what I shouldn't know,
And with a pain more real than that:
Wanting the house empty,

The room lamp-lit, and,
Pressed against my ear,
The wireless set, tuned to
The shortwave band,
Hoping for a message from
A vessel in distress
That no one else could hear:

'Mayday Mayday Mayday,
I'm sinking fast,
My only hope is you.'

At Elm Grove

The grass held home of the sun all day,
With no sound except a bird moping
In the trees. Frontier of shadows.
Over there is the road. Cars stray
Down it sometimes and the sound grows,
Then fades, and the boy stops hoping
Someone will come. And no one does.

Open cries of summer air the air.
His brother only. Sun clouds. A breeze
Darkens out of them and the light flees
Down the driveway. No, no one's there.
So he goes in. The kitchen curtain sways.
The clock ticks, so does the turf fire.

Not knowing why, he opens the door,
Kept closed for strangers, to the parlour.
Dark red velvet chairs, shaved tight.
The dust lies waiting on the plush.
For him it rises, like a guest,
Then slows and wanders in the sun.

The boy feels a weight in his chest
Of years that are past not yet begun.

DRUMCONDRA

The heavy trucks and buses mount the corner
Of Whitworth Road and crush it till it cracks,
Crush it crush it crush it till it cracks.
No right-angles in Dublin any longer
The traffic insists. The traffic attacks,
The pavement sinks, subsides, hunches its back.
Its mica mourns, starstruck, dressed in tarmac.
Exhausted gas exhales, ex-oil, ex-fauna.
The air is bony, a crematorium.
The meat-stink of stale petrol, burnt off, lingers.
And here the future tangles, flesh-flies trapped,
Wasps in wax, maggots in a honeycomb.
A crossed and fissured palm with spiderous fingers
Clutches the nail, unable to adapt.
Diesel it is idealises us.
The map of Dublin is in the hand of Jesus.

ELVIS IN GLASNEVIN

No kisses are harder to remember.
Any night will bear witness to that
With a rolling dustbin and a black cat.
Elvis is singing Return To Sender;
Most of the stalls are closed; the fortune teller,
Down on her luck, has taken leave from fate
And closed up shop; the candy-floss seller
Twirls a final cloud, like himself, soft and fat;
The dodgems clump together, sparkless, duller
Than the neon stars, turned off, grown cold.
The last ghost train bursts out, it has no freight.
But the barely formed kids are so carnal
And bewildered in the half-dead carnival
That it seems natural to have and to hold,
And though the fact is our paths have not crossed
And no kisses are hard to remember
Everyone like that tonight seems tender
And so what if, like Glasnevin, we're lost.

December night, a dog barking,
This ugly house, the torn chairs,
The mantlepiece crowded with things,
The unsilvering mirror in the unused room,
Have entered me with longing goodbyes.

The cold starred garden where
Farewell is not leaving the lamp
In the lane – its 'so long' lasts
All night, even to daybreak –
The walls which no one climbs,
Brambles grow under them now,
Bare apple and plum trees,
The iced greengage,
Its life given up.

So much suffering unknown,
So much distance the gift.

SONG IN A LOWER VOICE

Drinking coffee from a paper cup
I hurry down the hill to work.
A Christmas postman, that's my job.
It's six o'clock, pitch dark, I'm late again,
But I don't mind. I start to walk
More slowly and to sing out loud
Beneath the trees on Mobhi Road.
The hill is steeper here and diamond cold
And yet despite the hour some windows are
Lit up. Glasnevin jewels in the frost.
What's going on I wonder in these beds –
Are people making babies with the light on or
Are they just made anxious by the dawn?
In any case I sing out louder still
That love like this will surely come my way.

On Griffith Avenue – twin rows of trees
On each wide path – the sun comes up,
The sky grows pale, enamelled at the rim,
And now it's all a rush: a Merville Dairies
Milkman jostles his frozen bottles,
A marvellous sound, and in a cloud of steam,
The milk-horse chews the grassy verge
And takes her ease outside the church
Of Corpus Christi, lit up for first mass.
A dozen or so old people straggle in
To wait upon an even older priest
To dodder out and change a wafer to
The body of the god who made the world.
I doubt the miracle myself but not the fact
Of people getting out of bed for it.
But now I'm late to sort his birthday cards

And so I hurry on and in a lower voice
I sing for any lord who's listening.

ON CLAPHAM COMMON

I lie down in a rented bed
And go to sleep. Old walls, new shadows.
I'm on my own at last, thank god,
The dust is shaken off my feet.
Does everybody feel like this
Some time in life: adrift, cut loose,
Estranged, but free, anonymous?
Once I was afraid to leave the house,
But sleeping with you taught me
That love wakes up where love lies down.

Coming down the stairs next day,
I breathe the odours of another's home
(Floor polish, face-cloth must) and stop.
Known corners to someone else
Are opened to my eye.
Being here, I'm theirs.
Then, out on the sun-confining street,
Lost in the map of London,
I am truly where I am,
Though I carry no key,

And I lie on the grass of Clapham Common
For an hour or so, past the hours of business.

Drops of water drifting down
Through the sun
From the factory roof
Becoming a bright spear.
How slow!

How slow?
Thirty-two feet
Per second per second.
That's the law of falling.

And I too am its subject,
Hostage of the most,
Target of the least.
Beyond mercy nothing is mine.

Always a fool.
In the slow rain
In the sun.

How far away how far away
Is the field over there
Full choked with yellow weeds?

Go through the open factory door
Walk past the girls picking frozen fruit
And singing on the grey
Conveyor belt

And even the bright spears
Are far away.

Nightshift Cleaner

The vining machines empty and stop,
No more roaring and clanking,
And the power-hoses are coiled up loose
On their hooks as the dawn breaks.
The sloping yard runs with water
And everything I've washed is dripping,
Even the steel rafters in the roof
That I aimed up into just for the arc of it.
The factory is like a salvaged ship,
Sunken by night, brought up by morning,
Streaming, its lights still on.
And only then do I notice the silence –
The sun rises low, the buildings stand out,
And this is the coldest and quietest
Part of the day. One sound continues, though
Unheard before: the freezer in the shed,
Juddering faintly. Then it's lost again
As the real day begins with trucks
Far off across the town approaching,
Piled high with peas cut fresh last night,
Their intense perfume a well-kept secret,
And I lean on a brush in the yard
Pretending I have something to do,
Sweeping when I see a foreman's white coat.
Then, after breakfast in the canteen,
Breathing freely the warming air,
Going home to bed as the town goes to work,
I feel I can go anywhere
And have already been there.

PENSÍON ALCOY

To be played upon you must be empty
To be empty you must be open
The *pensíon* is empty
And the window is open
And outside the birds open
The clear spirals of their throats
And the warm wind flutes through them
A song of retreat that repeats
In the shadows
And all day a whole laundry of air
Has been dry-washing the grains of dust
Until each one gleams in anguish
And the hair-thin cracks in the gleaming tiles
Hold only those worlds that escaped

This wind too teaches the trees how to dance
Like negroes across the beat
They know what it means
They would walk away into silence
If they could
Because the wind doesn't know what it's doing

When the sun goes down the air
Stops
It is dumb-founded
The shadows come out then
They spread out long and thin
Freed from their cypress parents
They know they own everything
Everything they touch belongs to them

Behind the back of the afternoon
They flowed in through the windows
Like liquid animals
And slowly advanced down the cooler corridors

Now they have invaded and occupy
It's dark
The shadows have opened their eyes
And are waiting

The owl on Tibidabo's piney hill
Hoots his warning
And raises melancholy wings
Over the mouse he's killed

It's dark
The house is empty
The corridors are silent
The wind has gone

To be open you must be empty
To be empty you must be struck
As if you were a gong

Outside the window
The window is open
Its window is also open and a thousand more

And suddenly there is no more Mr Lynch

FOR MYRIAM K.

Adipose tissue, body hair,
I've got enough of both by now,
Though once my belly was hairless
And my chest was muscled thinly;
I was like a young god – or that
Was how Myriam described me –
Walking through the waves at Sitges,
The beach outside Barcelona
We'd take the bus to in the heat.
I was wondering at the time
How I'd escape, but I knew too
She was watching me tenderly,
So I let her. I allowed it.
All – all! – of twenty-four I was,
Loved by a woman of forty,
Who lifted her blouse to show me,
Wildly, wildly smiling, her breasts,
All white, with their sensitive prize,
Hints of inward reward exposed,
As we sat unseen in the sun
Back on her *atico* balcony.

On the beach or walking in the streets
We kept our distance, or she did:
This young god was less a trophy than
A secret prize, to be enjoyed indoors,
And besides, classically caught
And transformed into an object
in and by her helpless moment,
His mouth was blistered all over with
A raging dose of herpes …

And you – she is you to me now –
Had just come out of hospital
After an operation for
'a female complaint' (something simple) …
Well, I remember a sun-gloomy room,
The pure sheet they covered you with
And the electric tenderness
Of the nurses who knew I was not
The nephew you said I was,
And showed me, briskly, to the door
As you were readied for the knife.

But what we wanted was to go
Indoors and that is what we did,
No matter that it was too soon,
No matter what the doctors said.
There you showed me all your body,
All of it brown except your breasts
And that one other 'secret place'
Which they had revealed, scraped and reamed,
Where inner and outer join,
That bed-raggled purse which was
So purple-dark at the edges
It looked black in the shadowed room.
There I, outside, was able to
Go in and be showered by love,
The vault falling, corrugating, drenched,
No matter how undeservedly …

Well, I've got breasts myself now,
Hormonal hair grizzles my belly
And gut is a word I know about.
I'm nearly forty years of age,
I know the way into women,

That steep narrow night-gorge
Men try to balance upside-down in,
But I'm not proud about it now,
Or at least proud as I was then.

Myriam, will you forgive me?
A forty-year-old man is not
An Apollo and now I know I'm not
And can never be again to you
What you were once upon a time
To me, although I wish I was.

I Breathe a Drug

I breathe a drug
And what I call it is
The air.

The war against the war,
Against the waste of things,
Gives way to awe,
The poet's useless pity for
The Oh in everything
That fights against the law
And fails.

What brought all this about?
What makes the poet think
He has it in his power
To bring his moment out
Of time and burn it in
To someone else's hour,
To call the laws of sequence false,
And send you walking through
The blueness of an evening town
That yearns for going out
For fear of staying home?
Well, that was done to me and now
I want to do it in return.

The town knows what is meant.
It's covered with a sheet of doubt
Imperial in width and length,
And on it all the drops of neon light
Are sequins, like the tears
A youthful woman sheds the while

She's lying helpless on her back
Beneath her friend the moon.

The moon is glazed with waiting.
The town has emptied out.
But still the traffic lights trip through
Their declaration of unhuman rights
And still the streets say Yield.

Yield. Give way, give way.
Our best weapons cannot be used,
But what use could we put peace to?
When you kill you cannot
Get rid of the body. Someone always
Knows where it's hidden,
Even if it's only yourself.
But when you give up and surrender
You forget you are a warrior.
Will I go out or will I not?
The choice is free but forced.
It's written in default.
Neither of them wins.
Either way, victory or defeat,
Ends with a sigh,
Threatening the walls with doors.
And look, here is an open one,
Closing now. Go out, go out.

THE NETTLE WAY

The light on Killiney beach
all day it grows and grows
until it's time to darken
and then it goes
home into itself.

The waves sparkle then
under an immense sky
and a still warm moon.
The waves are brighter than
that floating stone,
they rustle together
like silk excited to speech.

The paths on the cliff
start breathing in the dark
a sharp nettle scent as if
the way to go was a warning,
and the salt air,
like a dumb thief,
enters you and tries
to speak to your belief
that being alive's
a secret you must keep,
or sink.

So close the door now
And think.

PAN AS SERVANT

A man with a slice of bread and a hat
In his hands knows that to rush
Would be a crime. But he can't think of much
Else, juggling with this and eating that.

Every day, he thinks, and even in the night.
He closes his eyes and sees where the trap is,
How the rigid day allows his flight.
But oh, he thinks, if I live and nothing happens.

THE CONFESSION OF JUDAS ISCARIOT

I confess: orgasm is the spark
That stops the fire. All it does is burn
For going and for going out. The dark
It backs away from since it cannot turn,
Kissing this cheek, then the other one.

Before you came I knew the way to crack
The folded female code. How was it done?
My spine was what I did my spying with.
The bark-stripped branch I hung from climbed my back.

The others – there's no point denying it –
They craved the fall, it brought them on to shiver.
But you, you turned your eyes on me afraid,
And I, I had the price of Christ betrayed:
I sold out for thirty seconds of silver.

In the Top Room

The sun comes in the window
And finds you out.
Everything that joins
Goes into hiding:
Elbow and groin,
Hidden and back,
The iris, flocking, contracts,
Eyelashed.

You are thinking of me,
I am thinking of you,
And you will do with me
As I will do with you.

The body's secret parts,
Where shadows always are,
The sun deepens them.
Stiff lock, soft rasp.

The rest of the room
Is blazing too.

With a sigh,
With a sigh that is
Almost a gasp,
We start.

Outlaw

I looked into your eyes and saw
The reflection of another man.
It was not to me your kiss was given,
Not mine the neck your noose had caught.
So why was I the traitor then?
What I hadn't wished for,
To be the stand-in for a star,
A better class of criminal,
Was your idea it seemed of heaven.
So I played the part the way I ought,
Or rather had to, at no great cost
To myself, it has to be said.
And this is how, I thought,
Found in a stranger's bed,
That Billy the Kid was lost –
But he was sleeping when
The sheriff shot him dead.
I did better than him.
I looked into your eyes and saw,
Don't stop, this is the law.

OUT AND DOWN

A moth just now, a piece of the world with wings,
Has risen up to this top floor window.
You see, what starts in the mind ends in the body.
Its jailer's the air, it has the thickness of glass.
Ours are these, mouth and skin and fitting parts.
I'm not, you know, well balanced for nothing,
But don't touch me there (it's too high up),
Anywhere else but don't touch me there.
Your feverish venereal resignation
The moth blundering, so dumb, against the glass.
At a loss for words, thinking of you, I go
To look out and down. The yard is filled with wings.
We've called suffering pleasure far too long,
Our lives are fleeting through these ghostly things.

BROKEN AGAIN

You sink down low in the bed
Until you're sexless.
So this is where
Your high thinking led you
And left you.

And was it even sex
That mental struggling,
That physical juggling,
With certain modes
Of spiritual undress?

Or that last pained call
As of a bird giving up its all
In a trench on a cindered star
To the final semi-cruel caress?

Yes, this is it, this is it,
Even though you're indifferent,

Broken and then
Broken again.

INVITATION TO SIN

'Sin in order that you may seek forgiveness.'
G. Rasputin

Because you are flesh you will,
So you should. Weak, stiffened,
Bright eyed, whose breasts are full,
Be loose, undisciplined.
Throw off your clothes and with
Them let what rules you fall.
Afterwards my hand's breath
Will bear you back your soul.
The risen rose because it fell.
The holy spirit's odourless
Before the lifted dress.
The uncommitted sin is hell.
Your musk, downed there, is heaven.
Give in then to be forgiven.

SCENT PRINTED

Weary with pleasure and weary of it,
Still drunk, dry-hot in the hot city dawn,
He has come home, blind-scaled the stairs and gone
To throw water on his face. Eyes, forehead,
Cheeks flood with cold. He mouth-sucks the torrent
With hard sex-greed. And afterwards he's drawn
To the blueing window. There he stands to yawn
At the day. The fingers that smother it
Smell of salts, the female-scent of torment
And submission, which pass here for pleasure,
As if the ocean gave up its struggle,
The battle won, the spoils not left behind.

Far off the roof lines sharpen under pressure
From blueness, acid-etched. First the needle,
Then the burn to cut away the ill-defined.
The sentimental prints as sweet fuck-all.
But still her scent persists, it permeates
His skin. He goes to bed, ripping the sheets
Back with a sea-slashed sound, sexuicidal.

PASS AND IT SHALL BE CLOSED

Look at him in the empty street, the square,
He feels he cannot enter it and only the air
Rushing slowly in the wind and the warm sun
Beaming through it to a point can beckon
The way to the waving trees and the bushes
In the locked park. And listen, a thrush is
Asking the ocean is it deep and how
If the sea turns out not deeper than the sky
Then who would say I love you less would lie.

But she is already in the next street now.
Before him the gathering corners seek to go.
Behind him it darkens. Here is the snow.

PANIC

Panic is our common language
Falling not falling by inches

Inches inches

Completely dead electric day
When you can't even laugh at love

And we go to bed in the afternoon
Completely sexually frantic

Pastoral Moderne

Twisted into unusual positions by hangover,
Two in the front and one in the back,
They drove that Sunday out into the mountains,
All hedged and ditched, it seemed, by lilac –
As in madness, the most obvious became the only.

There was a different shrub one of them thought
Might be 'white lilac', so they stopped
And broke branches off it. Elder flowers
They were. And all the rest were hawthorns.
They blamed it on the whiskey in Searson's.

Back in Ashton's the third one said,
'At least you can drink the stout here',
And they did, although the young woman –
'Don't mind her, she's driving' – stuck to whiskey,
And then Howard came in and as if the place was empty
Someone said, 'Howya, Howard! Any cocaine around?'
In such a way that all three of them started laughing
Wildly, like the branches outside in the car,

Since you don't ask Howard for cocaine out loud,
Out loud in Ashton's. Ashton's of all places.

Toppling Toppling

The tired night gives up
The sense of the night time outside
And the stilled town
Is swallowed up by the black spider
In the blazing white bath

The water rots in the taps

The moon is a weightless stone
Kept floating only by its mass

The towers incline
As the traveller approaches

O have pity

THE END OF THE AFFAIR

In the yellow weeds on the green sea bank
The butterflies made wild descriptions of the air,
As if at every turn they'd hit something hard,
And across the bay the massing thunder lowly grumbled,
As if to reprove existing things for what they were,
And then the rain came whistling like an old-style
Messenger boy indifferently delivering news of the dead.

After the shower the streets of the old town
Had an inland smell, slaked dust, trodden pine,
And the gutters were filled with clear water,
And the well which they'd told us was bottomless
In its diminishing drops kept on saying it was
Wrong like a bell wrong fainter wrong wrong.

HE LIKES HER CLOTHES

He likes your loose black dress
With the loose red velvet jacket over it
And the dark cherry-coloured hat
While you sit smoking straightbacked
On the wooden chair in the kitchen
Anxious to get out of here,
And also the long red tee-shirt dress
That you sometimes wear in bed
With the neck-buttons undone.

He notices then that your breasts
Are less girlish than they were,
More like any woman's used to bed,
Used to their being kissed and admired.

He likes the way you dress,
Though breasts is a shocking word
Joined up with used to,
And he would like it all the more
If only he could look as I do
On our desire and what occurred
To it so long ago.

A LATE HOMECOMING

I'm a publican, the man at the door said,
Do you know this girl?
I found her lying on the street.

Yes, I said, I know her. Thank you very much,
You're very kind. Saying all that twice.

He was young but old-fashioned I guess
Because he called you a girl,
And he said he was a publican I suppose
Because he had seen a good few like you,
Stitching the breeze to the district,
And he knew that that kind of street
At this time of night
Was no place to be seen in or found on
After hours and when he did
There was nothing else for it
But to lead you muttering home
And find the right house if possible.

THE DEVIL CALLS

To the man who made the nuisance calls –
Sex-filth for you, silence for me –
I first said, Ah, you pathetic little bastard,
But that was exactly the excitement he needed,
So the next time I cackled in a frightful way,
And hung up. Immediately he called back,
So I whispered, Boo. Boo boo boo.
Three times tonight he put the phone down
As soon as I said hello.
If he rings again I'll just say
Bad dream bad dream.
Why am I shivering?
Why are the stairs up to my flat
So worn out so brown so empty
So like the inside of a dead bone?
It's the devil.
The devil is in the city and he wants me
To know he has no one to talk to.
In the end I'll say, Kill yourself kill yourself
I'll be with you at your death-bed saying
Kill yourself.

Tonight when I picked up the phone
And said, Bad dream bad dream bad dream,
There was a pause.
Then the penny dropped into the slot
And a voice from the country said,
Hello!
Is Phil Fortune there?

HOPE AGAINST HOPE

As if insomnia and loneliness
Were human errors only, but terminal –
While the homosexuals parade
By the night's brilliant pool,
And the revolutionary smokers
Of marijuana hide out at home,
Turning the pages of time and space
Cut up as science fiction comics –
This midnight truth has truth
Written all over it
The way glass is etched with glass
In case you'd crash into it.

The weight of being awake,
This once and forever
Eternally unescaped from,
But with all its glories reduced
To the slurred click of the electric clock,
And even that glory is reduced
Which is like looking deep into water
When the looker too is water.

Insomnia and solitude breed two evils:
Moonshine and sarcasm.
Barbed, wired, grave-stoned, lime-lit,
Half-alive but all aglow,
I float without an edge,
Or the benefit of orgasm.
Hope, said Coleridge,
Who lost it,
Is the parasite of woe.

NOW

Now he remembers her saying that sex
Was simply – well, not simply – too disgusting.
It was a bang-bang job, a rabbit in
A cheap magician's hat, a bag of tricks
She wouldn't pull him out of, slick with wax.
For him it was the act he'd put his trust in,
A drama of star-showers, silken, rustling,
The slow curtain to the world's quick climax.
'And I was pure then,' he thinks, 'for fuck's sake!'

Forsaken, cursed, her magic just a hoax,
She vanished in a – hoop la! – puff of smoke.
Goodbye Miss Fridge! Farewell Miss Snowy Spine!

Years pass. Then, unexpectedly, they meet
While walking on a busy city street,
And suddenly the subject of these jokes,
More bitter than forgotten, changed by time,
Is you, and what is yours, this kiss, is mine.

A Child of Memory

My memory reproduces small things,
but each one them is
a child of the whole memory,
as if it wasn't chance that blew
the buddleia seed into the valley of
the abandoned building
and allowed it grow along the parapet
above the crowded street
where you as you
passed by on your own
going nowhere that I knew,
each drop of the rain on its flower cones,
now that the sun has come out,
confining a speck of city dust,
and what I loved most was your loneliness,
your caustic soda eye, harsh as jails
but fully aware of relative distance
bushing into it –
though I saw you then
looking down at the ground
and away to one side
as you gave the coin,
as if not to look meant
not to be seen

and that's enough for love
although the child is
a bastard with scabs
begging for money with

a Black Magic box.

You Came Back

When you came back
I was frightened
Because I had forgotten
The way you are
As if one could forget
A child impaled upon
A spike

And as you were
Standing there
In the uneven room
The tip of your cigarette
A dull dot in the dark
A red because declining star
That fell with your hand fall
The part of my mind
You'd been hiding in
Turned out to be the floor
Lifted up as a wall.

At the End

I was living inside
what things are made of
and my mind was still
when something black
with pathetic eyes
rose up in the room
out of the fire place
and I was frightened like
a dog in a silent storm

In the end I knew I would end
with my bare arsebones
propped up by coffin boards
in a hole on my own
with no pride and no friends

I was dead inside
what things are made of
and you came back and were
I don't know how not surprised
by that kiss those eyes this stare

THE ONLY REST

The only rest you know
Is the rest you know
Will not answer
Your tiredness.

In the next room one lover
Followed by the other
Makes sounds which are
The follow on to sleep,
Followed on by sleep.

And here you lie on
The far side of the wall,
Hearing the muffled sounds,
And then no sound at all.

The only love you know
Is the love you know
Will not forget
Yet has no memory.

KNOTS

The best thing is lack of
The lack of what you can't get.
The worst thing is that this
Knots into pure hatred.

The purity of yearning
After what can't be had –
Your pity for her, made sad
By somebody else – turns bad.

The secrecy of your virtue,
And the fact that what is good
Means having to be silent for good,
Starts something burning in you.

You half-see the universal
Where the oil-stains rule
And the jags in things
Function like kings.

The end comes when you don't need her,
When you organise your thoughts
And see not hate, nor love either,
And this not even in the knots.

CHRISTMAS DAY FOR AN ENDING

'My back hair, look, I don't know what it is
But it's becoming like a small girl's.'
Very feathery I felt it,
And the curve of your neck.

My Christmas nieces, their hair's like that,
Their warm necks and their feathery hair.
They embrace my legs and I'm laughing.

When I think like this
I want to sleep forever.

THIS OR IT DOESN'T MATTER

I call this hole in the air my home
And ask what dreams of the future could fill it.
Something swarms up the stairs in the dark,
A quick slow-motion holocaust.
But then she's there. And we start to talk,
Until, wordless, into nothing my nothing spills it.

One thing only – a tiny drenching drop –
Floods the whole empty edifice with light,
And what it's called is, 'This or it doesn't matter'.

THE TEA CEREMONY

Making tea in the morning
You love, or observe,
The exact ritual.
I'm lying warm in your bed
And you're barefoot in the kitchen.
(When both are habitual,
Love and observe are the same.)

One slice of toast with marmalade.
One cup of tea. One cigarette.
Me getting dressed.
You in your old kimono.

I kiss you lightly and go out.
Sometimes I even come back for more.

But now, I think,
That's where the trouble started:
The pleasure corrupted the joy
As super added spoils the man,
I got the habit of my habit,
Though I don't blame myself.
Oh no, I blame the Mitsuoko,
Your perfume, on my clothes,
It was too much for me,
I had to have it.

SHAPELESS

Clear mind, slaked body, rain on the window,
And opposite a cliff of houses so
Close from this top room there's no street between,
Though beneath us a whistler goes by unseen,
Not knowing that above him we're naked,
One of us awake, and that our clothes too
Lie tangled on the floor, just as jaded,
Thrown off the track, a disguised clue
That at the start foretold the story, how
We would end up, their future, here and now.
The future is all over the place, done for,
Behind us, as odd as the backyards are,
A sprawl which no one planned and, so, looks far
More like the way we really think of things
Than does the street, too formal to be slack.
I guess ahead and see a man who sings
While walking through the house from front to back
To wash his face as if he was made out
Of air inside the rain that sluices pure
The city summer night. After the rout
The battlefield is quiet, nothing moves.
The war's more real like this, the bathroom blues,
He thinks, more deeply felt. And so it proves:
He can't sing now. This window or this hour,
This way of being poor, he didn't choose,
Yet here he is, the victor, in their power.
He sees the streetlamp in the ill-used lane.
Its so-what halo bends the straight-ruled rain
Into a bow. This light comes to obscure
Its purpose in the shadows of the yard.
The wall, the ramshackle shed, the buddleia bush,
They know it now and, suddenly disturbed

And showering notes out of its nest, the thrush
Knows it too. The man bends to slake my thirst.
Clear mind, how wild we were, I think, at first.

PERPETUAL STAR

Never to meet again
In the way they'd once done
And yet he had decided then
To be devoted in the old sense
Discovering lateness early
Unremedied and irredeemable

Never to be really met again
Although remaining always in sight
Like the 'perpetual star' in the evening

IN VAVASOUR SQUARE

Almost a tramp, the man who wears a flower
Always in his lapel fell down the stair,
The single step, into his rank parlour.
Luckily he'd left open the hall door
So he was seen down the long corridor
And rescued by some young men passing there.
No one had any idea who they were,
It being midnight, a cul-de-sac, and rare
To see strangers out in Vavasour Square
At that or indeed at any other hour.

Earlier his lodger, a young mother,
Was hit by her husband with an armchair
And ran crying and bleeding from the ear
To the kind people in the house next door.
Their son, on crutches, his leg in plaster,
Brought her off to hospital in his car.

In the narrow front gardens of the square
Rose bushes thrive and, cut straight as a ruler,
The hedges grow higher. It's lonely here.
There's no traffic, no other traffic, near.
But what an old, old mistake is the air,
Exhaling the day's heat when it's cooler
So that the roses bend then slowly rear
Their blued pink heads, as is the night's desire.

FIRST NIGHTMARE

I drop my work and hurtle up the stairs
Because I hear her crying in a way
She's never cried before, a sudden spray
Of otherworldly screams, caught unawares
By – nothing worse – the first of her nightmares.
She's new to this, I think, and cannot say
What she has learned, that there is hell to pay,
And from its depths a hopeless demon stares.
While fast asleep and safe, she felt the ground
Beneath her slip, and now she's standing up
Behind the bars that keep her in the cot.
I lift her out. She throws her arms around
My neck and holds on tighter than a cup
Its handle, or a strangling child the knot.
How strange! And stranger still to realise
She doesn't know my name. She isn't mine.
I could be any mirrored ghost with eyes
Whose gaze she's seen, whose weight she's borne before.
I carry her, as water carries wine.
She is the miracle I'm looking for,
But what she is I am the spectre of.
There is no she. That she is you, poor Clare,
And you, some day, will die, and not of love.
The thought of that, it drowns me in despair.
I clutch you like a straw and start to hate
The floating life that you were born to lose.
How lourd death is. But then you press your cheek
Against my own and it's both warm and cold,
And for this once I understand our weight,
As downy as the skylight's evening blues,
And how these attic walls, like me, grown weak,
Can bear it too. One day – I hope you're old

For both our sakes – you'll wake and find I've gone
Back down the stairs and can't come up again,
But when that happens, do remember this:
That on the night when you first felt the pain
Of other-dread, which can't be woken from,
You had a father's, I a daughter's, kiss,
A functional emotion that lives on.

DETERMINED POEM

After millions of years, no, hundreds-and-thousands
Flung all over the place, a cosmic trifle,
At last we know what the birds are saying, 'singing':
This is territory, this food, this sex, and here is
Something due purely to the physiology,
The formal structure of the avine larynx.
The robin whistles now, it sends four notes flying,
Then three, slower, to mark the gaps we cannot hear
In the first flight. I spread four fingers, index them ...
But maybe it was a blackbird, a thrush, a wren?

And then, as the seagulls cruise over, a flurry
Of notes too quick to count by the ear shakes the bush,
And a mild breeze blows, and drops of the recent rain
Fly off both of them. New silence. New sounds carry.
Overhead the seagulls pack and revolve, heads turned,
Garden in one eye and blue in the other one.
Silently they wheel. After the meal is the time to squawk.
It's nothing to them, the 'beauty' of the garden –
Nothing to the garden either, so greeny-blue, lit by
An intense local light now that the sun has gone down.
The sky is clear of clouds, the hedges dull and glow
And the grass is a different hue, more emerald,
Because its absorption rate is that much swifter
Than the privet or the berberis with its private suns.

The window stiffens; all its molecules jelly tight;
And the unveiled air smells of where the rain went.
Out in the street a single car parps, wise with hints,
This street that has only the sky for name-plate.

These numbers number less than the stones on the beach –
Over there on the far side of the railway track –
Milling towards a finer flour. They're trying to bleach
Themselves of any tint, their geometry is pebble-dash,
Their Euclid rules a line and ruins it all at once.
The sand has an engine too, its motor is the ocean,
And what the waves know they write out in white
On black, or fawn on beige. To them it's all the one.

It's darker now. The bird's throat-surging musical
Gurgling is put away for the night, determined
Not to be, as we are, unreasonably, happy.
The world is not the world's laws, or even its friend,
And the language, how could it hope to correspond?
But the solitary car parps and parp-parps in the street.

COLD SORE

Herpes, Hermes of the inward hive,
Wings its brute heel from my brain to my lip,
Breaks out and quickly tents a blister there.
Then through the tissues of the house I hear
The child cry out and clogging footsteps go
Across the darkened passageway to her.
I heard the call, but didn't answer it.

A herald with a message from the spine
Emerges silent, glum, then rawly gleams
And weeps before he roughens, dulls and dies.
A herald with a message in the house
Is fed and then sent back into the dark.
The page is bare. Which one of these am I?
I strike a match. The smoke is Mercury.

Ruffian boy, a nude and beardless youth,
The perfect athlete, with a scab, a crust,
A dead spot on his lip, has dreams of home,
Of bringing milk into the honeyed dark.
But all he sees is this, a stone-floored room,
And all he hears is Fame, its vulgar cries.

In love with whatever there is to love,
Weak as it is, I am,
And like an almost domesticated bird,
I build my nest in a ruin.

BETTER TO MARRY

I stand at the window and see
What was near me now is far.

The contract, signed to keep us apart,
Contracts and wires us together.
I thought what we were formal for
Was for the sake of trinity.
That's three fors:
You, me and a third force
Which has no personality.
But now at last I know nothing can stop
The shock of us being twogether.

Behind my back the black music revolves
In our vertically pure white room,
Singing marriage is necessary
Even as butchers require knives,

And I plunge through your hell
As if its walls were made of water.

Il Picciolo – the Stem

Mosquito whine, and mint and fennel cut
Outside the window, flame not far away,
Dryness rising and the sense of glut.

The itch of sex, the bite that through the day
Cannot be salved. A drop of pine tree sap
That thickens. Silence of the new-mown hay.

The moon is high. The porcupine's quills slap
And click as, waddling up the path, she sniffs
Its glow. Half-globe, half-black, half-white, a map
That acts as camouflage – until it lifts.

Indoors your hackles rise. That leads to tears.
They're ended in the shower. Hieroglyphs
Of water fall and globulate ... These years,
All of them, all thrown away as scrap,
Are mint and fennel now, ungathered-up.

A STORM IN TUSCANY

This shapes his life – it does much less for you.
All his experience he brings to bear
On something it takes seconds to read through,
Which raises then an eyebrow or a sneer.
His typing fingers stop. Against the grain
They palp the shaven corners of his mouth,
And this takes up an hour, and more, of strain
In which he weighs two words. He chooses 'drouth'
To slake his thirst; a wholly foreign place,
Whose language is thick cotton on his tongue,
To be his home in speech; a house that's old
Beyond its years to make his feelings young.
But now, dried-up, he feels instead his face
And idly wonders will the weather hold.
The fevered silence makes him lift his head.
Outside the birds have suddenly grown still;
A hazy stubble thickens round the sun;
The air is like a beaten sheet of lead;
Then raindrops spatter on the window sill;
Far off the thunder fires its warning gun;
The lights go off; he finds a candle butt;
The wind begins to lash the olive trees;
The shutters bang; he fights to get them shut,
And as he does he smells sweet hay and sees
The lightning bolt. The gutter overflows.
A match is struck, and then this candle glows.

FOR DANTE AND LUISA

Dante holds the pigeon that I've bought
And shows it to the girls. Luisa then
Goes off a little way and wrings its neck.
There is no pause between its life and death.
While Dante makes a fire, Luisa strips
The feathers off the breast. The hens eat them,
They're rich in calcium. The fire's to singe
The pigeon's stubbled skin. Just two handfuls
Of summer grass are needed and a match.
The purplish body passes through the flames.
We're hidden in a grove of trees above
A hollow deep in Tuscany. It seems
Ideal, but Dante keeps the hen-house locked
And hides the key beneath a different stone
Each day, because Arcadian neighbours thieve –
I'm not surprised but think, there's someone in
The village sees, I'm sure of it, the smoke.

This afternoon, at home, in privacy,
I hack the pigeon's head off with a knife,
Then finger out the guts and throw them through
The window to the cat. They vanish in
A timeless gulp. The mad cicadas' drone
Goes briefly up a pitch to mark that pause,
To spike the straight relentless heat.

The bird is young and needs no stewing, so,
I stuff the cavity with sage and cloves
Of garlic crushed with salt, massage the breast
With olive oil, and then I roast it till
It's crisp without and slightly pink within.
Well-buttered cabbage and half-baked

Potatoes mound the plate. I eat them all,
And suck the bones. But neither wife nor child
Will join the greasy feast – they look at me
As if I were a Vandal slumped
Across the table in their Roman home.
I notice then, while toying with
The carcass, that the crop is plump with grain.
A pigeon has no teeth and I forgot
To clean it out. Alarmed, I pause.

And now dessert. I think of something sharp
And sweet, and kiss my women till it's dark.

THE FIREFLY AND THE COIN

A firefly flew into the room,
A coin fell off the bed.
One rang, one wandered, through the gloom.
Which made me turn my head?

The glower plotted up a cone,
The coin a spiral drew.
Neither acted on its own.
I paused, and so did you.

The spinning money got the drift,
And yawed from side to side.
The gleaming intervals grew swift.
Then both together died.

The flashing ceilinged and went out
Just as the whirring stopped.
Your hand, moth pale, lit on my mouth.
And so the penny dropped.

THE HOOPOE'S CREST

For the Jankowskys

The hoopoe's crest was made of gold,
Which made it valuable to hunt,
Although its inclination was
To make its nest amongst the foe,
And so it went to Solomon,
Who understood the way it spoke,
And pleaded for his wisdom's knife.
The gold, that burden of its head,
He turned into a feathered fan,
And off it flew, its song unchanged,
Desiring still to nest with us,
But weighted now with memory.

That year a couple nested in
Montisi's burnt Siena fields
Close to our faded ochre house.
Each morning and each night
I'd see one standing on the track
As if on purpose to be seen.
As darkness fell they seemed to come
Ever closer to our windowed light,
That golden opening through the trees
We hardly knew was beckoning –
But still the 'idle boys' chased them
And they recognised a gun.

That year you came to visit us
And stayed in La Casella, which,
Although nearby, was out of sight,
A rambling farmhouse up the hill,
And there you learned their call so well

We didn't know the difference
Approaching through the olive groves.

That gold has changed to feathers now,
A vanished fern fined down to air,
And it's two hours to midnight on
The final day of Eighty-Six,
And yet, with memory in it,
I hear the hoopoe calling still
And almost everything it seems
Is possible again and hope
Comes ever closer back to now.

DREAM SEQUINS

The lash of the nocturnal south-west wind
Impels the heavy waves against the cliffs.
By dawn they're thunderous. No one hears this.
The yellow gorse blots, greyed by dew, grow dim.
The leaping hare's unseen. He leaves behind
A broken track, dashed through the foggy grass.

In here it's pitch. Out there the cleared sun lifts.
The sleeping village gleams. Shops shine, sequinned
Sidelong to the harbour. Taffeta shadows
Contract erotically, shrink for the light.

A mild breeze comes at last, bells curtains, goes.
In the room butterflies panicked the night
With paper clouds. The walls now bear their weight.
And the man with the whip lets out his breath.

CLEAR LIGHT AND THUNDER

Clear light and thunder
Are here now, so let us go under
The trees and turn to each other.
The valerian dims
And the burn of its pink swims
And reigns on the walls' falling kingdoms.
The streetlights crackle
And spark in their glass tabernacle.
First they're violet but when it's dark they'll
Stop their fluttering.
It is dark, but the ring
Their haloes make can't yet be seen.
It's cold. You shiver
And I startle: we have to live here
Like rocks in an unseen river.
You put out your hand
Like the night's first moth and
In your throat, grown taut, your breath
Lets out just an 'o',
A birth-sound those who leave the womb know.

Listen: the thunder, far away.
See: the clear light of no longer day.
They only hint they know this too.

CARILLON

A blunt carillon of bells
This foggy frosty afternoon,
The block of the shed, its sharp edge
Skinned close to by the icy air,
And further off the trees, the road
Where it dips before the corner,
The dull brown roof of Marine Lodge
Unusually red – these things
Become in mist too much too far
Too near and where, too, are the bells?
There are no bells here.
A slight, slight delusion.

And then – it's night – the infinite.
A fine rain hanging over Strand Road,
Hardly seeming to fall at all
Through the one streetlamp's needle ball,
Downy in its aureola.
Worry. Worry worry worry.
My hair capped with it wets my hand,
The final hour hourly approaching.

Final hour, the last's laugh,
The perfect part of all that's guileless,
How must you be treated?
The wet hedges tremble their held cascades,
Their duped hearts still green in the dark.
But something rustles and stirs,
As if in a bottomless well
Some mammal swam, real inches long,
Lost in imaginary years of light,
Worried about how long he has waited,

How to get out, a trapped thing thinking 'up',
Amazed, hardly aware it's walked away,
As the fine rain thins, then thickens.

The corrugated iron roof rings
As the downpour pours down on it,
And a big loud train, indifferent
To indifference, thunders past.
Now it's now.

My Mother's Death

The night before you died, that night of nights,
When asked who should stay, you said,
'I want Mary, I'll hold on to my Mary.'
What words those were. What words
Did you hear then when Mary and the rest of us
Had gone? Those of the aeroplane
Roaring that the sky is this size and the beehives
Beneath the trees in the gardens of
Nazareth House know it too, they buzz off
Because they have no other choice?
Earlier I'd seen the plane and heard its noise
From the window of your room,
And you were so nearly blind and confused
I told you what it was, in case not knowing
Would frighten you. Was that the purpose or
Was I the more afraid? We were transposed.
But even then you had more poise.
My brother asked, 'Can you see me, ma?
It's Philip here.' 'See you?' you said, eyes closed,
'I've a pain in my face looking at you.'
Ah, that smile – all joy to be the mockery of fate.

Then your dying gasps: chain-stroke breathing.
How is it I never heard of this before?
No, I was told, it's Cheyne-Stokes'.
Two doctors I suppose who were well-used
To death rattling and rasping at the weak links
Of its captivity, too long drawn out,
And since it had no name they gave it one.
But no, the sister said, she knew the signs,
You would survive the night. She got it wrong,
And we went home. But that's OK.

I don't hate to think of you alone there
As she ran down the darkened corridor
To ring and then returned to place
A lighted candle in your claspless hands.
I only wish to know who thought of this,
To hold between the going and the gone
A waxen thing consuming its own flame.

And thus, by driving fast, Joe reached you first.
Eight minutes he said it took him and still
There was a faint pulse left, a fading throb
Transmitted to, withdrawing from your wrist.
And when I arrived his car was parked
Up on the footpath and he'd climbed
Over the gate, which had been – afterwards –
Opened for the rest of us. That word
Between the dashes is intended there
Because it still extenuates its length here:
We'd come too late but after all,
And still, we were in time.

And now Van Morrison is singing on
The radio, 'Have I told you lately
That I love you?' This is not urgent news:
The question's answered just by being asked,
And for the living lately can be made up for.
What's urgent now for me, though too well known
And too apparent to be spoken of,
Is that all natural death is humble, and
Because it's also simple has no pride,
And life for that reason makes a mock of it,
The way you always did, until at last it can't,
Just as the way you lived you died.

THE JEWS ESCAPE

Ghostly the house,
Ghostly the way out,
Down the unlit stair.

Brighter the street,
Darker by far.
No passerby is there.

Then a sudden shout
Stuns the quiet.
Its cry is *'Juden, raus!'*

No one can deny it,
They would tie us to their posts
If they got the chance.

And they will. But not tonight.
Tonight the door is open,
The yellow stars are ours.

Why is everywhere closed?
Your answer is a glance,
You too are in their power,

You too are chosen.
Behind us is the door
And silently it closes.

Bad blood is everywhere,
The whole wide world is frozen.

By a heavy eternal blow
It has been laid out.

So let us go
Like ghosts

And slow.

POSTMATURE EJACULATION

I went to sleep and saw the fortune teller.
An ill-famed house it was, a whorish dream.
Among machines she loomed, a mad machine,
The place a Palace of Amusing Terror.
This she, a pro, was sitting on a chair,
Sidelong, skirt high, her white legs crossed and bare.
When I spoke to her – or did I? – she knew
Exactly what it was I meant to do.
OK, she said, and bonelessly stood up.
All limp I put my penis in the cup.
The slot through which the future's cards come out
Was made of brass the light rolled gold about.
The whore approached, as if she thought she must,
And ringed me with a hand that smelled of lust.
Her other hand flicked through a picture book,
An album in which photographs were stuck
Of soldiers, businessmen, clerks, all upright,
And every one of them his eyes shut tight.
But none of this had sex that I could see.
I said, Is there nothing with the family?
These words are true, but then just as I spoke
My body shuddered fiercely and I woke.

ENTROPY

Who-kills-spiders thinks of his house
Mortar-crumb by mortar-crumb pulled down,
A silken web, a felt strand of air,
Rasping down this jagged rock
To a ball bald of mountains.

The spider-killer is me,
An island the size of a man
In a sea the size of a woman,
And when we kiss tonight
History trembles, one iota at a time,
And you begin to cry.

Launched out, unbelayed,
a salt drop let drop,
What height will we not fall from?
One state winding down to another state,
The boredom that allows
Something only human to occur.

A bird sings out of contracting shadows,
The sky sweet water and a star like wine.

Who-kills-spiders his fate
To give a spider kiss,
Feeling immortal and wishing for nets,
And only in that mesh his death forgets.

A cry in the house becomes
A cry in the street.

The street silvers off
Into the sea-paths of the moon.

Tonight every night trembles

FIFTY

The clock ticks on to twelve.
I have a minute till I'm 50.
I have to stop remembering –
I've reached it now –
And turn to writing poetry.
Earlier, Camille came in
Before she went to bed.
You're only 49, she said,
And 364 days old,
And kissed me tenderly.
My life was in her mouth.
Her life was in my heart.
What more is there to ask?

What more is there I ask,
And think of where I've been today:
To see my native place,
The house where I was born –
It's been converted into flats –
And then my parents' grave.
I read their epitaph: Better Now,
Added since my mother died,
A thing she used to say
And kept on saying
Even as she lay dying,
Her mind almost gone, blind
And in agony, defiant.

Amongst the pebbles on the grave
I laid a sprig of laurel leaves.
I'd plucked it from a bush
In the Botanic Gardens

In passing unthinkingly,
And found I had a use for it.
Such is life for poetry,
Or vice-versa: the accident
Is afterwards the signpost.
But how explain the rose
On my desk in a tumbler?
As I was going out the gate
I passed the railinged shrine
Where Tom Moore's song
The Last Rose of Summer
Is commemorated with
An offshoot of the flower
He'd been inspired by.
A tight-furled bloom was growing there –
Remember, this is February:
The Last Rose of Summer was
The First Rose of Spring –
And so I nipped it in the bud
And brought it home.

What is it trying now to say to me?
I've stopped remembering.
It's twenty past one, far too late,
And I am 50 years of age.
The lane is darker than the sky,
And yet I see it's ended with
A laurel bush, the first, the last
Of roses and an open gate.
It seems I've reached that final stage
When final means the start of it
And starting off involves goodbye.

A House Divided

The structure does not seem
Able to support its weakness,
And of all the beams
Grief is the one that best
Outlasts its house.

Though marriage is more or less
A jerry-built contraption,
Solid as an ice-cream cone,
Unlike grief, which is concrete,
Still, when all's sad and undone
And what seemed iron creaks,
How can it not be seen
As the ideal, the roof-joist,
The foundation stone,
And, however makeshift
A joy-function, the last post?

Beyond the other laws,
When everything else is lost,
Collapsed because
Of its inbuilt flaws,
It endures and hurts the most.
You scream. I scream.
We all scream for ice-cream.

And it used to be true
Of our house, fixed up when
Broken down, as of any other
Sunny suburban slum:

Someone who is in the club
Is preferable to someone
Who can do the job.
But it's not true now.

Too Bright for Hell

A sickle moon shines small tonight
Between the ragged, scudding clouds.
The bushes and the trees heave too.
What's rooted moves. At any rate,
These Siamese twins must separate.

A dog barks. Over city miles
Another answers. Where are the crowds?
The late-show cinemas are full.
The End is nigh. They'll empty soon,
Their engined curtains stir and swoon.

The gloomy vandals roam the streets
The way it seems I lived with you,
And passing cars go whoosh with fright,
As if charged off your violet power,
The weak force, felt this midnight hour.

What happened here? Something turned dull.
That shameless dual thing which whiles
Away the time, a spot of rust now eats
In solitude. Too bright for hell,
Our story's still too dark to tell.

THE LAST WORD

The first sound was 'Oh'.
Its pain became
The bread of song.
A bad French pun. Ho ho.
And yet it's the beginning
Of wisdom you know
To be wrong.
But the more you suffer
The worse you behave.
Another old joke:
I'm going home.
Why?
I forgot something.
What?
I forgot to stay home.
Oh.

THE IDEA IN LONDON

The things that go into the brain
And never come out again.
The idea in London
That each of its lights
Is for someone
And the railway stations
We pass through without stopping
Are for the dead.
Poor England, full of names
Worn away out of history,
Disappearing into comedy,
And all down the length of the line
Its gnomic houses, back to front
And perished at the edges,
Like myself
Heading for an unknown bed
In a carriage lit by marsh gas,
Consulting a tattered
'London A to Z',
And then a passing train
Like a woman ghost
Fleeing through the night
With her mouth open
Crying 'O' with a sound
Like tearing silk,
Leaving a scream behind her
Going into a scream before.

In Passing

As I come out from here
I'm thinking what I thought –
'Though nettles throng the path,
The way to go is clear' –
The street-lit garden's calm,
Too bright for hell,
Too dark to tell.
The scent of nettles cut
Inside my head is matched
By what is real and crushed.
By living underfoot
I earned a single alm:
The gift that past
And now will last.
Such pride. I am at most
Alone. This, fame allows.
But as I near the house
I'm startled by a ghost.
It's black and grey, a breath
Of mist the face,
Too dim to trace.
It's you. It's you, stood still
Upon the gravelled path,
More stony than the truth.
Jesus, I cry. That thrill,
A second long as death,
Is gone. Then I
Just pass you by.

MYTH

Daughters, to escape
Their 'family of origin',
Leave home, cross a magic bridge
And change their nature.
Their father sees them as deer
And tries to shoot them.
They tell him who they are.
He lowers the gun and says come home.
They say no we have to
Crush you with our antlers
And anyway they are too wide
For the hall-door.
But when at last they do return
The house is empty in the sun,
Mother has gone south or north,
And, there now, fatherless,
The door is wider than it was,
Or wider than they thought.

DRY TEARS

I woke this morning in the dark and cried
A man's dry tears, that waterless relief,
Not making something foreign to itself,
As windowed rain can sometimes stare a street
Too hard and stern into a pendant drop.
A quarter of a century had passed
And suddenly your ghost had reappeared.
I knew the reason why: a friend I loved
Had struck your memory a passing blow.
That hardly mattered then. What mattered was
You had grown older in a way unknown
To my experience, and all this brain
Could do to fill the years of in-between
Was dress you differently (an off-white frock,
Too youthful for a woman of your age)
And give you work related to my own
(A job in films, the sort of craft that gets
A disregarded credit at the end).
That was all. But still your eyes were true
To life, exactly captured, narrowing
Before you'd say, 'You seedy little man'.
You didn't get that chance, for in the dream
I said your name – the least of what you need
To hear the most that I could say – and as
I did you leaned your body over me.
Within the different dress I saw your breasts.
They looked a little slacker than they were
But lovely still and tender and untouched.
And then I woke dry-crying in the dark.

THE ROOM

I stood in the darkest corner of
The Room
And thought, Well, this is what you wanted,
Isn't it? The water-heater panted,
Over-breathing like a respirator for
The coughing man next door.
The breast of chicken-in-the-bag
Went bad because the *frigo* was unplugged.
The grille was hanging out the back
And every time the motor clicked it clanged
And rattled till the thermostat,
Gone mad, would cut its throat,
And so I'd pulled the plug.

I walked out of the darkest corner of
The room,
Walked up and down and smoked,
And saw the supermarket bags
(Not nearly filled but tied),
The single knife and fork,
The single pot and pan, the double bed
That one had rumpled, the book by Lorna Sage,
Bad Blood, who died, and thought,
But this is what you wanted, isn't it?
Freedom, France, a furnished room, *en suite*
(A leaking shower in a booth),
A bed that's not your own, or made,
Which you had better lie in, soon, again.
Well, I think, at least the rent is paid,
Though something must be added when
I leave for heat.

IN MEMORIAM MICHAEL HARTNETT
d. 13th October 1999

Fox-bird, gone to ground,
Found his dovecote rest at last.
Fox in being cute, a pet,
Yet unbiddable, openly hidden,
Caught out in what he had to say.
Bird in that he was only seen
Outside the window flying past.

Belovéd friend of many women and men,
Unimaginable father, childless seeming, yet,
Uncanny, with offspring all over the world.
Come home, children, across the unwalkable water.
Say but his word and your heels shall be winged.
There is no better way
To reach this inward islandman,
His soul nailed through,
Forever on the last, calm, unhinged.

Good food, bad jokes, worse puns, much laughter,
Often drunken, and 'the cheapest
Possible cigar', all, all –
But not enough – to pass away his time
Upon the cross of loneliness and worse.

What is there left beyond
His Angela, his family, his friends?
His poems. We call them home
Because they weren't his.
Let them go wild again
And dumb be fox and bird,

And empty lair and nest,
For lovely Michael's gone
And who but they can show –
His ghost become a brightening star,
The brightest and the best –
How kind and sweet he was
Who was so harshly blest?

OUR BEST QUALITY

For Mary-Beth Hughes

Mary-Beth said tenderness.
Just that. No more, no less.

This wasn't rocket-science,
Nor was she making of it
A claim to a clean breast,
And there wasn't any hint
In her plain grey voice
Either of defiance.
It was said flat, calm.

Already – I didn't have to be Ovid
To feel far away from home –
Having made no choice,
And thereby failed the test,
I felt hot, that I might faint, alone,
Without, thinking of it.

But Mary-Beth said tenderness.
Just that. No more, no less.
And I thought, this feeling's not unknown,
But it works both ways: soft pointed,
Hard felt, heavy, piercing the breast.

9/11

A wound in the side of America,
A golden day and two broken ribs,
And the best of our hopes now is scar-tissue.
Seen from outer space
It's only a wisp of smoke,
But with it comes the awful thought,
We got what we deserved
Because we've gotten it.

Out of an Afghan cave a Saudi girl
Steals off into the dark. Her heart throbs,
It's ragged, like a rosebud gnawed by a wasp.
The sound she heard that frightened her
Was joy and thanks to Allah who is All-Merciful
And tumbles towers and beautiful boys
And girls of all sorts. The word travels fast.
She loves her father in the mountain cave,
But she had imagined his world, this world,
To be natural, kind, companionable.

We too imagined it to be in sympathy with us.
It is. And it is not.
My God, to live in America you've got
To have two jobs – is this fair?
Do we have to hurt this much just to be here?

Months later the space ship returns.
A tweezers has picked out the dust
From the hole grain by grain
And now it's clean.

And the men and women down there
Are invisible as they always were,
But the answering-machine had been left on
And in the dust of the now fixed rain
Of its silver-brown molecules,
Immovable on the tape, but permanently disturbed,
The strangest of all messages remains:
'I love only you always John Doe.'

And so, and so, as ever we did roam,
The shuttling craft drifts on,
And through the near light speed atoms' fear,
Through the dust of John become Jane,
Risen up, all wholly souls, become one
By rising, through all worlds, wrenched, blurred,
Through 'love only you always', we hear
What Ovid says in his erotic poem,
'These are the wings that must bear us home.'

THE DAY I DIED

It rained all day the day I died.
Everybody else
Took it for granted,
As if such a backdrop
Was intentional,
Only to be expected,
Like the ringing of bells
At a wedding or a funeral,
Like an old song the tune
Of which is forgotten,
But it wasn't and it isn't
Ever meant to stop,
It is sent to be as near
As we can get
To being eternal.
So I took nothing for granted,
Though I was confused too
And hardly noticed
The people as they came in
And went out of the room;
I had other things on my mind,
It was hard to say what
Other than dying,
Which involved that
Only as a physical sensation –
Not present and not frightening,
I was by then long used to
The feeling of falling,
To heart leaps, fainting,
The absence of plans –
But the constant light rain,
The showering drip

And the electrical click,
Like the oxygen machine,
And the no-nonsense hands
Wiping cool my brow,
And the pure white cloud
Clinging to the tip
Of my favourite mountain,
The women's one, as in the song,
Which was pointed out to me,
Though I couldn't see it somehow,
Except in my mind's eye,
Where it was immense,
And no distance at all
To Tipperary, which is what
I saw then and still hear –
All of these things seem now
Dividable from the experience,
Or for the living, now or presently,
Who are not dying, should be.

THE MURDER OF MARGARET WRIGHT

*The following is an extract from 'Angry Heart Empty House', a
poem of 1,560 lines composed in the Aisling form, a
traditional dialogue between the poet and Ireland envisioned as
a spéirbhean or heavenly woman. The poem deals with three
emblematic crimes, Bloody Sunday in Derry in 1972, the
murder by the IRA of Patsy Gillespie, the so-called human
bomb, also in Derry, in 1990, and the murder of Margaret
Wright by loyalists in Belfast in 1993. One man, Ian
Hamilton, the 'Ian' of this piece, was murdered by his own side,
and six other people, one of them a woman, were jailed for a
variety of offences related to the murder. Nonetheless, when this
section of the poem was to be published by the Royal Hibernian
Academy Gallagher Gallery as part of the catalogue for an
exhibition of paintings by Gene Lambert in 1997, it was
withdrawn at the last minute on the grounds that it might be
libellous of those who had been found guilty by the courts. The
entire poem was published in The Ring of Words, the anthology
of the 1998 Arvon International Poetry Competition.*

'I'll tell myself your second tale,
It is the story of a young
And voiceless girl, a nightingale
Who died because she lost her tongue.'

But then she stopped. A dreadful fright
Took hold of me. Oh speak, I cried …

'My heart is full of Margaret Wright,'
She said at last, 'and how she died.
There are some things so alien
To light it's best to turn away
From seeing them, and this is one.
This darkness has nothing to say.

I'll speak for it. I'll sing for her
The song of cemetery birds
And as I do, her mouth, that blur
Of worms, I'll cleanse with eerie words.'

And now out of her mouth another voice
Came out, a Belfast girl's, the childish kind
That once upon a time perhaps had sung
That Albert Mooney said he loved her, all
The boys were thinking of her. Out it came
As white as snow, but infinitely sad
And cold, as hollow as the rings she wore
Upon her finger bones, more mournful than
The little bells that tinkled on her toes.
Old Johnny Murray said she'd die
If she didn't get the fella with the roving eye.
She'd got her wish. A man had fixed his gaze
On her and she had died. This ghost now spoke:

'My name is Wright but I was wrong:
I didn't fit, I couldn't work
At any kind of job for long
Before my brain began to jerk
And fizzle in my puzzled skull.
It played with me, like cat and mouse,
As if I was invisible,
A spirit in an empty house.
Those epileptic spasms split
My life in two: my home was good,
I was my mother's favourite,
A window in her widowhood.
And we believed. I was a Prod
And proud of it; my room, kept clean
And neat, displayed my faith in God:

Beside a photo of the Queen
I'd framed a picture of a lamb
Embroidered on a linen sheet
And round its head I'd stitched the Psalm:
Thy word's a lamp unto my feet.
I was, I hoped, a child of light.
And yet I also knew the dark.
There was another Margaret Wright,
A woman driven by a spark
Within her head to run away,
Get on a bus downtown and then
Go wandering, get lost all day
And in the night be found by men.
You know the sort? No matter that
I hardly knew my name or where
I was, there'd always be some cat
Who liked a mouse and didn't care
If it was too far gone to play
The game of loveless sex, that death
In which the self, a willing prey,
Allows the beast to catch its breath.
But even in their claws, the eye
That looked at them was cold, a glare
That drove them off; the only sigh
They heard a sob of pure despair,
The kind a prisoner makes at last
When he accepts the only way
To force his present be the past
Demands he throw the key away,
To tunnel in instead of out,
Draw over him a crushing quilt
Of stone, and from its dumbness shout
'My only innocence is guilt …'
And yet I could throw off that chain.

Somehow, some day, some night, I'd wake
And find myself at home again
And feel once more, once more, the ache
Of being in my mother's arms,
Forgiven for the hurt that I
Had done us both – her love still warms
The grave wherein my bones now lie.

But then, one final time, the fuel,
That petrol electricity,
Ignited in my brain its cruel
Need to burn and, burning, flee.
I fled. I didn't say goodbye.
For me the house was empty too,
Get out! Get out! its frantic cry.
So, like a moth on fire, I flew
Into the night. The streets, ablaze
With haloed lamps, were dark to me.
How long I baffled through this maze,
The Long Kesh of our geography –
That block is theirs, this one is mine,
Or once it was – I cannot say.
But all the same I knew the line
I had to take, the safest way
To go from south to north Belfast.
The Village there, the place in which
Somehow I ended up at last
That April night, is only rich
In Protestants, a people poor
But generous to strangers when
They feel their hearts, like mine, are pure.
The only thing I can condemn,
Their plate-glass silence, soon was cracked –
I'll tell that story bye and bye:

It's still the only violent act
My broken heart is mended by …'

She stopped. That woman of the air who had
Been speaking for this woman of the earth
Could not go on. I knew the reason why:
The time had come for Margaret to tell
The story of her death and even she,
Who'd opened up the tomb and rolled its stone
Aside, as poetry is meant to do,
Had reached the furthest limit of her art.
At last she gathered up her strength and from
Her mouth the smaller voice came out again,
But slower now, the sounds it made as dark
And heavy as a flock of graveyard crows.

'The place I'm in is painted black.
It's windowless, a blank concrete
Flat-roofed shed off a cul-de-sac
Down at the end of Meridi Street.
A flute-band is supposed to use
The hall for practising. In fact
It's just a shebeen where cheap booze
And dope are sold. And now it's packed …

'I'd knocked. Behind the chipboard door
I heard the bolts being drawn.
They opened on a muffled roar.
A tattooed bouncer loomed: Come on,
He said, come in. And in I went,
As white and silently as snow.
The smoky air inside was rent
By flashing lights. The vertigo
I felt and all my drunkenness

Had deafened me. I didn't hear
The roaring voices fade or guess
That I had changed the atmosphere.

'At first they only circled round,
Like bashful partners at a dance
For debutantes, but I just frowned
And stared like something in a trance,
A creature hypnotised by light,
A mouse that doesn't run away
But waits, unconscious of its fright,
Until the cat comes out to play.
A little tap, a tiny nudge
From one big paw I felt at first
Upon my arm. I didn't budge.
A face came close to mine and cursed
With stinking breath into my ear:
I said, it said, what is your name
And what the fuck are you doing here?
For who I was and how I came
To be in hell I had no word.
Perhaps I said, I'm feeling sick
And said it so he thought he heard
Me say, I am a Catholic.
I must have made that sort of slip.
Why else would he have screamed so loud:
We've got a Popehead in the kip!
A Popehead? Me, who was so proud
Of being a Prod! They prodded me
At first, the way a Judas goat
Is goaded till the pack can see
The way is open to its throat.
And like hyenas too, the craft
Of teasing me to death was fun:

They howled with joy and as they laughed
They gathered in a ring and spun
Me like a parcel in a game.

'The females of the species too
Were keen to prove they were the same
As men, or better, since they knew
The way a woman's pride is hurt:
One held my hands, as if to dance,
Another lifted up my skirt
And stripped me of my tights and pants.
Oh Jesus, in your final loss
You weren't as cruelly mocked as me.
You weren't as naked on the cross
As Margaret Wright was forced to be.
It was my sex that drove them wild,
And so I'm glad for memory's sake
To say I never had a child.
How could I bear the endless ache
Of being here if I had borne
A son or daughter on the earth
Who'd have to think of me and mourn
The day that I had given birth?

'It seemed at first that mocking me
Was game enough. But when I thought
They'd seen it all the mockery
Got uglier. One joker caught
My hair and then another one
Began to slap me on the head.
But when I lay there still, more dumb
Than snow, they hit me till I bled
With fists and billiard cues, the shaft
They'd broken off a sweeping brush

And others clubs. And still they laughed!
How comical it was, the gush
Of blood that spurted from my nose.
How funny too the way I crept
Across the floor without my clothes.
They laughed so much they almost wept.

'But then, as if they'd hit a wall,
They stopped. The screeching music too
Cut out. Across the crowded hall
A rippling wave of silence flew
As fast as light but heavier.
They held their breath. I never thought
That air could be so weighty or
So still. A glint of steel had caught
Their eyes, a gleam off something black.
Just as I saw it was a gun
They bagged me with a plastic sack.
I knelt there like a naked nun
And tried to pray. But no words came.
How could I beg for mercy when
I didn't even know my name?

'The crowd began to breathe again
But now they didn't laugh. Instead,
Like beasts who've scented blood, they sighed.
I felt the gun against my head.
For Christ's sake, Ian, someone cried,
Let's get the fucker out of here.
The store room's safe. We'll do it there.
I tried to rise but, weak with fear,
I fell again. They grabbed my hair
And dragged me out across the floor
Into another smaller room.

I heard a click – they'd locked the door.
And then they hit me with the broom
And with the billiard cue again,
And with each blow they asked me who
I thought I was. I was insane
With fright and suffocating too
Inside the sack. I couldn't speak,
I couldn't tell them anything …'

And then? And then? And then?

'And then
I felt the gun against my cheek,
But didn't hear the deafening
Explosion that the bullet made.
Four times they fired. Four waves of light
Mixed up with blood and smoke were sprayed
Against the wall and Margaret Wright
Was dead. I died as silently
As any woman ever did.

'But that was not the end for me.
My killers still had to get rid
Of what was left, the rubbish in
The tattered sack, the bloody slush
Of bone and brain. A wheelie bin
Was what they used. They had to crush
Me into it. What could they do?
They couldn't get the lid to shut
Because one leg stuck up. They threw
A coat across its dirty foot,
Unlocked the door and wheeled me out.
The hall was empty now – a cloud
Of cigarette smoke whirled about

The lights to show how fast the crowd
Had fled the bullets' leaden roar.
Among the broken glass the clothes
I'd worn were scattered on the floor.
The only sound, the stereo's
Electric hum, droned on and on.

'My killers ran me down the road
Until at last they came upon
A terraced house. A streetlamp showed
Its eyes were blind. Someone had bricked
The windows up against the rain.
The place was vacant, derelict.
Beside it was a high-walled lane,
A narrow passageway, unlit.
They dragged the bin down there into
The dark and tipped me out of it.
One climbed the wall. The other two
Took hold and swung me to the top.
But I was slippery with blood.
They lost their grip and let me drop.
A nail snagged off the plastic hood
And then they saw that Margaret Wright
Was looking up at them. At first
They were so overcome by fright
They froze, but then with one last burst
Of panic and of rage they hauled
And shoved and pulled me up the wall.
There for a moment I lay sprawled
And then the catcher let me fall
Into the stinking yard below.

'The place was full of things like me,
Soft stuff in bags, a sodden dough

Of food and clothes but cushiony
To land in, if it hadn't been
Mixed up with splintered furniture,
The steely guts of some machine
And other bits of junk which were
So broken and so old they'd gone
Beyond the need for names, like me.

'But when the sun came up and shone
Into the yard it saw that we
Had settled down and made the most
Of turning rigid in the frost.
I was at one with them, a ghost
Who'd found a home by being lost
Among the homeless. Out of sight,
And out of mind, impervious
To cold, we waited till the night
Once more drew darkness over us.
Foot loose and fancy free and far
Removed from any worldly powers,
We waited for the morning star
And fused its innocence with ours.

'So, peacefully, the sky turned grey,
But then a stranger climbed the wall
And saw my face. I heard him say
Oh Jesus! Jesus Christ!, then call
For help – that name and cry belong
Together but their pleadings, meek
As they are, can't prevent the strong
From coming late and being weak.
But, still, they came. Nor did they laugh.
Policemen and detectives sighed
While someone took my photograph

From every angle like a bride
Who's just been married, blushing pink
With happiness – it was so rude
The way I stared and didn't blink
An eye although I was quite nude.
Well, that was that. Another day
Was done. Their gloves and plastic smocks
Were taken off. They drove away
In cars. I followed in a box …'

NOTES

First Poem: the Seven Dolours is the parish church of
Glasnevin. The old white-painted wooden church has
now been replaced by a black-slated pyramid.

At Elm Grove: the name of my grandmother's house,
outside Ballivor, Co. Meath.

Dayshift Hangover: the Ross Foods factory, Westwick,
Norfolk.

Nightshift Cleaner: the Fropax factory, Ware, Hertfordshire.

Pensíon Alcoy: the *pensíon* was in the Tibidabo district of
Barcelona, the hill from which it was said Satan tempted
Christ with the wonders of the world. In 1968 Tibidabo
was on the extreme limits of the city, but now a
motorway runs behind the hill.

Cold Sore: according to Everyman's *Classical Dictionary*
Hermes is depicted as 'a nude and beardless youth,
typical of the perfect athlete'.

The Hoopoe's Crest: this myth can be found in Gilbert
White's *Selbourne Diaries*, as can the reference to the 'idle
boys'.

Clear Light and Thunder: this poem has been set to music
by Jerome De Bromhead.

The Jews Escape: an almost entirely different version of this
poem was published under the title 'Ghost House' in the
collection *Perpetual Star*.

The Room: written in Cotignac, a village in the Haut Var
region of Provence.

Our Best Quality: written at the Yaddo artists' colony in
upstate New York. At dinner one evening a member of
the kitchen staff, who was doing a project for children,
asked the artists to say into a tape recorder what each
believed was his or her best quality. Mary-Beth Hughes
is the author of *Wavemaker II*.

9/11: the poem imagines that when the news of the attack
on America came to Osama bin Laden in his cave in

Afghanistan his Saudi daughter was with him. The line
by Ovid refers to Icarus.

The Day I Died: written at Yaddo in April 2003. The voice,
which is imaginary, is that of the artist Tony O'Malley,
who had died the previous January. Although he lived in
Kilkenny he could see Slievenamon, literally the
women's mountain, which is in Tipperary, from his
bedroom window.